All About Plants

All About

Seeds

Claire Throp

Raintree is an imprint of Capstone Global Library Limited, a company incorporated in England and Wales having its registered office at 7 Pilgrim Street, London, EC4V 6LB – Registered company number: 6695582

www.raintreepublishers.co.uk
myorders@raintreepublishers.co.uk

Text © Capstone Global Library Limited 2015
First published in hardback in 2014
The moral rights of the proprietor have been asserted.

Edited by Claire Throp and Brynn Baker
Designed by Peggie Carley
Picture research by Ruth Blair
Production by Victoria Fitzgerald
Originated by Capstone Global Library Ltd
Printed and bound in China by RR Donnelley Asia

ISBN 978 1 406 28440 9
18 17 16 15 14
10 9 8 7 6 5 4 3 2 1

British Library Cataloguing in Publication Data
A full catalogue record for this book is available from the British Library.

Acknowledgements
We would like to thank the following for permission to reproduce photographs: Alamy: Dirk v. Mallinckrodt, 18, 23 (middle); Getty Images: S.J. Krasemann, 19; Shutterstock: 2009fotofriends, 4, AlessandroZocc, back cover, 13, Charles Brutlag, 21, 23 (bottom), Daleen Loest, 16, Elenadesign, 10, Filipe B. Varela, 5, Jose Ignacio Soto, 22, Mazzzur, 8, 23 (top), Michal Zduniak, 15, Nikita Tiunov, 17, Photoexpert, 9, Pressmaster, 20, Rimantas Abromas, 7, Spiber, 6, sunsetman, 11, Thomas Klee, 12, Vitaly Ilyasov, 14; Superstock: Tips Images/ Maurizio Polverelli, cover.

We would like to thank Michael Bright for his invaluable help in the preparation of this book.

Every effort has been made to contact copyright holders of material reproduced in this book. Any omissions will be rectified in subsequent printings if notice is given to the publisher.

Contents

What are plants?

Plants are living things.

flower

stem

leaf

root

seed

Plants have
many parts.

What do plants need to grow?

Plants need sunlight and air to grow.

Plants need water to grow.

What are seeds?

seed

A seed is one part of a plant.
Flowers make seeds.

New plants grow from seeds.

Different seeds

seed

Some plants have lots
of small seeds.

seed

Some plants have big seeds.

Some seeds are round.

Some seeds have wings.

Spreading seeds

Some birds eat seeds.

These birds drop seeds
in new places.

The wind blows some seeds
through the air.

The seeds land far away from
the old plant.

Some seeds burst out of **pods**.

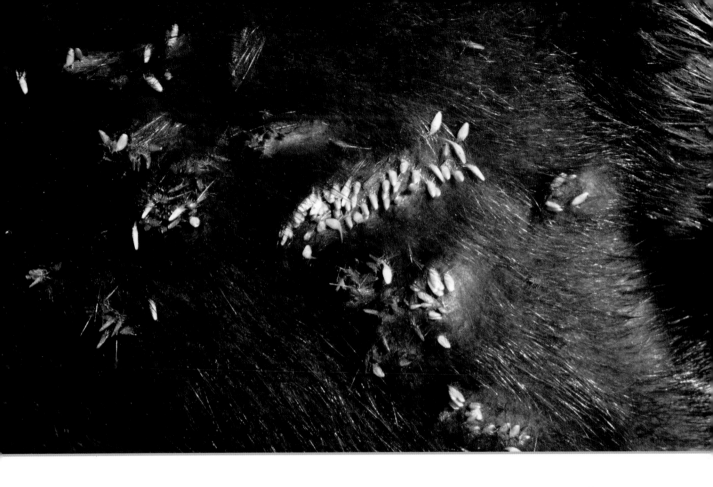

Some seeds hook onto animals' fur.
Animals carry seeds to new places.

How seeds grow

Seeds usually grow in the ground.

seed

root

They grow **roots**.

Plants need seeds

Seeds grow into new plants.

The new plants make new seeds.

Picture glossary

 **flower** part of a plant that blossoms and makes new seeds

 **pod** part of some plants in which seeds grow safely inside

 **root** part of a plant used to absorb water from the ground

Index

Notes for parents and teachers

Before reading

Find out how much children know about seeds. Make sure they understand that most plants grow from seeds and that most seeds grow in the ground.

After reading

- Gather a selection of seeds for children to investigate. Provide magnifying glasses for children to use to examine the seeds. Ask children to group the seeds by size, shape, and/or colour.

- Draw simple pictures of the sequence of plant growth on separate cards. For example, seed in the ground, roots growing, shoot growing, stem forming, leaves appearing, flowers blossoming. Make copies of each card. Divide the class into groups. Children can work together to put the cards in the correct order.

- Provide a small pot, soil, and seed to individual, pairs, or small groups. Demonstrate how to plant and care for the seeds. Allow time for the children to observe plant growth.